W9-BJN-174

CLASSROOM ROOKIE

By Ted Stevens

A guide for new teachers

Published by
Bread and Butter Press
1107 Dorothy Street
Lakeland, Florida 33815-4418

Edited by LaVerne Stevens

Copyright © by Ted Stevens 2004

Cover Art by LaVerne Stevens

All rights reserved, including the right to
reproduce this book or portions thereof in any
form whatsoever, with the exception of pages containing
forms to be filled out by the reader.

ISBN: 0-9630441-5-X

Library of Congress Control Number: 2004091389

Printed in Marceline, Missouri, U.S.A.

First Edition printed April 2004

Preface

There must be a couple of genes in the DNA helix that triggers an individual to teach. It is my belief that teachers are only motivated to teach from within their reason for being. Professional training and experience only temper the metal and sharpen the skills.

Teachers will communicate with others to help them understand what they need to know to improve who they are. A teacher is easily identified. They enjoy motivating others, are continually seeking information, will listen to problems and are driven to talking and illustrating until a satisfactory answer is reached and understood.

The term "rookie" is used to tag a newcomer to the game. A new teacher is a target for students, peers, and administrators. When someone enters a new field there are several ground rules that will intimidate, harass, and completely frustrate the rookie.

It is my wish that this book will help the beginning teacher understand what is going on.. It is impossible to cover all that is needed to know, but it should help set the scene for the coming venture. Everyday will be different and every student unique.

This book is for the "rookie", a title referring to the new kid on the team and in no way is it to be demeaning. It is a special time for any professional.

I was a "rookie" in 1958 in Ohio, I moved to Florida in 1975 and have been here ever since. My Bachelor's Degree from Baldwin Wallace College in Ohio, a Master's Degree from Michigan State University and various workshops and courses from Case Western Reserve, Bethany College, and University of South Florida helped to shape my training. ...but my students produced the teacher.

My wife, LaVerne, has continually encouraged me to write down some of the thoughts about teaching which I have shared with her. So perhaps someone will glean a thought or method that will help in their quest to teach and I'll still be helping someone to learn.

CONTENTS

Page

Preface

CONTENTS(cont.)

Take Five: The Professional Teacher

Anyone entering the teaching profession must realize that it can take *five years* to be ready to walk into a classroom and begin working with new students.

Since I have no way of knowing what grade you are going to teach, I have given a general description of the duties and expectations you may be facing as a member of a school system.

There is little difference between the lower and higher levels. In either case you are working with young minds and you have definite goals to meet. In any case, remain flexible and surprised at nothing. There are times when students over achieve and others that are no where near where they should be.

You must always work with the student at their present level and slowly move them higher. If you move too fast you will lose them and all that has been accomplished. I have often used the watermelon seed syndrome in similar frustrating situations; The more you squeeze the seed to make it comply with your wishes, the faster it slips away. Patience and a kind word is the best way for progress. Sometimes this word can be used forcefully to get the student's attention. Do it !

Here is how it goes:

The *first year* you will be finding your way around the school itself. This is done with the body posture and set jaw of self-assurance, because you don't want to be tagged as a 'new teacher'... but you're not fooling anyone. As the year progresses you find other teachers who you feel comfortable enough to approach for help and advice.

Along about this time you may have found the *two most important people in the building*; the custodian and the principal's secretary. They should always be at the top of your list.

You will be dismissing some of your pre-teaching tales and advice from ED 401 and replacing them with the *real story*.

Your past studies may have neglected to tell you about Student Rules of Conduct, The Dress Code, hall passes, office passes, interruptions for announcements and /or students are to be somewhere else other than your class. Then you have daily, monthly, semester and yearly reports on most anything. Plus all the staff, departmental, administrative, and parental meetings. This is usually topped with District Health and Safety workshops after school or on a workday.

In your spare time you can fill your bulletin boards with copies of rules, student information, bell schedules, fire drill classroom maps, rules for your classroom with the penalties for breaking the rules, rules for the substitute, student activity schedules, and most important is your name and what subject you teach on what day and time.

You must always be ready for the unannounced activity for all or a great part of your class to relocate and you are the supervising teacher for your students during the activity. Or the sudden opening of your classroom door with an administrator's curled finger directed to one of your students to come out for some clandestine reason perhaps never to be known by you.

Then there are the extra duties that are expected to

be performed. I have never really found out who assigns them, but your name will appear on one or more of the duty lists. The duties differ according to the age group of your students. The lower grades have duties called; bus, lunchroom (with your class), library, and sometimes P.E.. The higher grades are more imaginative with duties called: hall, john patrol, locker clean out, lunchroom(one half of class period), after school sports, breakfast, and cover(for another teacher's absence from class).

The duties will give you a chance to meet the students on their ground and a good chance to interact. You will get to know each other one way or another.

Your first year will feel like your teaching is out the window and all you are doing is trying to get ahead of the system. You are right, so get through the day and subject matter(see page 41 on Curriculum) and do what you can to keep order. You will just have to chalk up the first year to experience and promise yourself to do better next year. When all the punches are not coming from the blind side anymore, you will be ready for them.

Don't be like a "rookie" police officer and try to change the system by ticketing every offense that crosses your path. The key is to react to the level of the offense, and *you* have to determine the levels by your own experiences and no one does it from "go" with the right answer. The second and third years will begin to present order to the plan. You will start building your own lesson plans and seating arrangements(see page 13 on classroom).

By now you have some idea about how you keep the class attention on subject with fewer distractions.

You should concentrate on student interactions and

develop some plans to keep them from missing what is to be gained by being in your classroom. Be sure to have the time covered with activity both formal and informal. The students will plan activities you may not appreciate, if you have dead class time available.

Develop various types of tests to help you discover which type will complement your present style of teaching. Your style will change when you come to the realization that you may be testing the way you were tested. You may even discover some of the same terms coming from your mouth that echo your favorite teacher from the past. You will find the middle ground that includes the past as well as your own style. Don't fight to get it, and it will come regardless.

A "good" seating chart is never set in concrete. Keep it flexible and under *your* control. The tone of your class will be reflected by class interaction and not your wishes. Let everyone sit where they like and from then on separate the problems, but leave the rest intact.

There may be some problems that the students can handle by sitting where they will be attentive and comfortable without personality problems, *which you may never hear about.* Especially if you're working with the "puppy love" group. Don't take sides, just do your job.

The fourth year, begin to enjoy being the teacher. Maintain the control, improve the lesson plans, find some new ideas to make key points memorable and real to the student. Smile and laugh with the students. Ed401 told me not to smile with the class till Easter, I couldn't do it. If you are organized and relaxed everything should move smoothly and you will find the students moving with you, not because of you. Learn by the success of your peers not their own failures. Don't be influenced by the war stories vented in the Teachers' Lounge. The next day the same teacher may come in singing praises to the enemies of yesterday. It is healthy to complain, but don't take it to heart. Form your own opinions.

Some teachers ask for their problems by the way they react to the results of their own methods. I have found that a class will reflect the tenseness and frustration of the teacher and react accordingly. It is most important that you leave your problems outside the classroom door.

Year five, you should be excited and ready to start. You should have a plan from day one and a good idea where you are going. The year that I first felt prepared has kept me going ever since. I felt my senses leap, when I saw my name on my teacher's box and a feeling of comfort, as I opened my classroom to get ready for my day with the students.

If you haven't grown during the four years and feel positive about the fifth, then quit now. Many beginning teachers stayed with teaching with all the feelings of insecurity and lack of organization and they became unhappy professionals looking for a better way. My advice to every group of my graduating high school seniors has been that each person must find the type of work that he/she is going to enjoy and get up in the morning looking forward to the day.

One day I was walking down the hall and I heard students chanting and yelling from a classroom a few doors ahead of me. It was from the new teacher's room. He had just come to our system with a Doctorate of Music and wanted to start teaching this year.

I looked in his opened door and found him at his desk. He had his head down in his hands and was in tears. The students were jumping from table to table, throwing books and paper everywhere.

I was in my fifth year of teaching and my presence stopped the frenzy. All returned to their desks, cleaning up as they went. I must admit, I felt that I had made the grade in control.

I took the teacher down the hall to the office to the Principals Office and returned to the classroom until another teacher took over. I never saw the new teacher again.

Home Plate: Your Classroom

If you are fortunate to have your own classroom, you will certainly consider it your domain. To be a "traveling teacher" and have your domain located in your lesson plan book, the grade book, and your traveling case will be a test for your skill to be near Sainthood.

When the room is yours, you should have control of how it will be used. You are responsible for all that is put into it or taken out. All students are to understand what is expected of them when they enter and their behavior while they are within it. You have to establish an invisible line at the doorway and stand by your expectations.

Your desk is off limits to all students. All prepared materials are stored in definite locations and *available with permission*. **Teacher texts, answer keys, student information, grade books, all desk and master keys are to be out of sight and unavailable to students.**

Have a common place or box available for material to be turned in to you at any time during student movement. If you use a plan where students need to receive worksheets and turn in work, establish a zone of exchange.

This sounds like an unfriendly and restricted environment. It is. You must maintain a professional barrier between you and the student to do a professional job. Students expect you to do a good job and you owe it to them to stand by your rules.

"The Trap" new and young teachers fall into is to become a "buddy" by being funny, friendly, and permissive. These teachers want to be called by their first names, have favorites that they spend time with and tell stories during

13

class time. Students can have access to anything and want to do what they want. You can't blame the students. They all want to be considered grown up and can do grown up stuff. These students have leadership potential and want to bust out of kid-hood.

It is even more interesting to realize that the "buddy" teacher has lost the respect of the whole class including his new buddies. It will be just a matter of time . The trap will close and we will lose a potentially fine teacher. Perhaps in the long run this teacher will see it coming next time and get on the ball, but he will never do it with those who knew him when.....

You can enjoy your class, if you know that you have a good system of interaction. You can relax and be yourself. Teaching has been and can be a happy time in the lives of all those involved. This can be done within the roles of teacher and student with respect for each other.

To this day, I still refer to past teachers and professors as Mr., Miss/Mrs., or Doctor. Even when I later became a member of the Faculty at my first college. It really hit home, when some of my students came to teach in the classroom next to me and I was still "Mr." with a friendly smile. (one of those teacher paydays).

You are responsible for everything in your classroom: the furniture, display cases or bulletin boards, chalk or felt pen boards(whatever happened to the slate chalk boards ?), windows, window shades, heating and cooling equipment, lighting, speakers and alarms, all subject related materials, clock, computer equipment, video equipment, and there should be locks on everything.

Your responsibilities also include the health and

safety of the class, which includes: filter replacement on air equipment, first aid materials(check to see what you are allowed to do by law- The Good Samaritan act is not valid in many cases), all warning signs for areas where a student can come in contact with agents that will cause bodily harm, direction signs for drills(fire etc.), check heat and air controls, shields on overhead lighting, broken furniture, cracked or broken windows, loose wiring, faulty wall plugs, and the control of any object used in the classroom that could cause harm.

Your job is to report, in writing, to the office(keep two copies) about a problem in any of these areas.

Don't try to fix anything. You will be told it is not your job. The office has the responsibility to see that the problem is taken care of and you have done your job by reporting it. *But be sure you relate the urgency. Move the class from harm, if need be. Do the paper work later.*

In case of a student injury or seizure, be sure you wear the disposable gloves. You should have a list from the office that will give you the names(confidentially) of students with problems of which you should be aware. You may have to have some training of how to treat the student with seizures or other related problems. Even hypoglycemia or hyperglycemia could be a problem on the list. Never give a student any medication. All medication is handled by the office. *No student is to be carrying medication.* And don't forget the accident report.

One year I had a student come to me and talk about committing suicide. We were in the hall with students passing by. I listened as politely and calmly as I could and nodded with the inflections of her voice. The bell rang and she was off to class and I was on my way to the Guidance Office. The counselors wrote the incident and called her out of class. They instructed me to return to class and talk to no one about the problem, which I did.

At the end of the day I was called in to the office. I was informed that she always talked that way for attention and not to worry about it. She continued the rest of the year with no problems. Whatever caused the problem apparently was gone.

As a teacher and not a professional counselor, your job is to report all such comments or off the shoulder talk.

Don't ever assume anything.

Call the plays: Dress Code

Back when I was in the dress of the times at school, I wore a long chain with my house keys on the end. The chain hooked to my belt, went down below my knees and looped back up into my pants pocket. I wore my knickers below my knees and let my socks bag down. We had to wear a tie every Friday and the girls wore middy tops. I thought I was pretty tough! But my home room teacher was bigger and stronger than me. The loop was in my pocket, the knickers were above the knees, and my socks pulled up. If she had her way I would have had to wear two ties on Friday.

Through time the skirts went up and down, shoes were more expensive. Styles went wild and today you just don't know what to expect. Believe me school is the proving ground for the latest.

School Systems will spend hours and weeks setting up the dress code for their schools. We have the duty to see that the code is followed.
In this case no one wants the teacher to make any changes in the code and all are to conform. No matter how you see it. All is black and white and no grays.

Whenever I would find a problem with a student's understanding of the code, I would try to explain the social reason for the code request and give them a chance to contact home and make the necessary adjustments. I seldom needed to keep after them. If they wouldn't accept my judgement, they were referred to the office for the final say.

The reasons for the dress code should be known by

the staff. Not only are they for social suggestive reasons, but also for the student's safety(eg: flip flop shoes on stair ways).

Whatever the trend of the day brings into your classroom, try to react in a calm manner. Take the students from the classroom when relating the dress code violation.

Students will react differently when they are corrected in front of the class, than they will by a friendly word spoken quietly and forcibly in the hallway.

You may be getting smiles from students when you bend the rules, but they won't have the respect for you that you want. You're one of them and you're not doing your job. If you support your administration and staff, you can expect the same in return. If not, you will lose the control of the part of your job you most want to keep.

My classes, I feel, were happy to be there. We all knew what was expected from each other and it was reflected in the respect for all. It is a good feeling when you can work with students without the fuss about the things that don't have anything to do with the subject you are teaching.

It takes the light from the Sun 8.31 minutes to reach the Earth. When you think you are seeing the sunset, it really went down over eight minutes ago. It will be over 8 minutes ahead of where you see it all day long.

Most any star in the sky outside of our Solar System is not where you see it. It may have exploded thousands of years ago, but the light of the explosion hasn't reached your eyes.

On Time: Punctuality

Time seems to run the school. Not only for classes to start and finish, but due dates for work, tests, and grades. The discipline of doing what has to be done on time is as equally hard for the teacher as it is for the student.

There are prime dates for reports from the staff to the office. Don't be like the kids and wait till the last minute and not have enough time to finish the job. Start as soon as you know that something has to be done, finish what you can, and put it where you can see it or find it right away. As soon as you have the report done, make two copies of it before you turn it in. There is a ghost in school offices that will spirit reports into a never-world and blank the mind of everyone. When you find out that you had turned it in and no one remembers you doing it... you have another copy to turn in that you saved in your file.

It is usually a good idea to be by your door *before* the tardy bell.

If there is any trouble between students it will happen in the hall before the bell. Don't be coming down the hall from the teachers' lounge or late to school. If anyone is hurt, you may be considered liable. If you are going to be late, let the office know in enough time. Then they have the responsibility to cover the class and there are no surprises. (Don't do this too often).

As far as the class is concerned any work due at a certain date and time, is due. I wouldn't fool around with makeup work. Mark it missed. Grade everything! No check marks!

Everything turned in must be in the best condition *that*

student is capable of doing. Instill pride in doing a job well.(See page 43 on Homework).

You set the pace in or out of your class. Expect of your students the same as they expect of you. Don't work a double standard in dealing with time and work done. You are the example of a professional attitude and this is one of the major characteristics that you want to instill in young adults.

Dealing with time and doing what is expected are important lessons for everyone. If you, personally, have a problem with either of these characteristics, you will see an improvement in yourself as you work with the students you are trying to help. Students will carry these characteristics through the rest of their studies and will be the better for the example you've set down for them.

TLC: Attendance

It is very important that you keep perfect records of student attendance. You may have a book given to you to keep daily attendance records. That book is to be secured at all times. **When there is any sort of emergency drill, that book must be in your hand.** The reason is that you must know who is in class at that time and you are to recall roll to see if everyone has left the building and they are accounted for.

This is law, regardless how other teachers follow this rule, this is one of the prime responsibilities of all teachers. Always be sure to cover yourself and do what is expected.

If you are keeping records on the computer, print out a copy when you have taken attendance and put it where you can grab it in a hurry. You should keep a file of all records in any case. As a general rule, it is a good idea to keep a copy of anything you send to the office or to a student's parent. Sometimes things get lost or misunderstood and a copy solves many problems.

You should also make a list of your students and include some way of noting health or behavior problems that must be medicated. Many systems will not allow students to self medicate and they must go to the office. The office or guidance should always notify you of students with special problems (eg: seizures etc.). *Keep this information confidential.*

A student's record of attendance may be called for at any time. They are used in court issues or by child agencies to protect the student. Some schools will suspend or permanently release a student with poor attendance. Make sure your records are kept up to date.

Your attendance is equally important to the class. It is hard for a new teacher to stay healthy when every sickness parades in front of your desk daily. Keep a supply of health aids in your desk.

Watch your class for signs of fever. Fever is the time of contagion. Any student that is sleepy, red in the face, sweat on the brow, and eyes at half mast should be sent to the office to be checked by an administrator and possibly sent home. You can not send anyone home, the office does that.

That goes for you too. As a general rule; every day you drag yourself to school, you can count on two more at home. Spray the room with disinfectant before the day begins and after the last class. Being a rookie, you can count on being sick at some time. The experienced teachers just seem to be bulletproof and seldom get sick. There may be several in the school that have had perfect attendance for years. They have built up their resistance and immune systems during their rookie days of exposure. Some of the kids believe certain teachers are just too mean to be sick.

Also be aware that some students have ways of feigning sickness to a get a day off. I know of a certain athlete in high school that had a normal temperature of @ 99.4. The school nurse would send him home if his temperature was over 100.

So while going to the nurse, he would run two long flights of stairs and go in immediately. Sure enough he was on his way, excused for the day. The payback was the leg cramps I would have at night.

Management: Discipline, Control, and Referrals

The control that you maintain in your classroom is your own doing. What you expect of yourself is directly proportional to the production of the class. When I taught, my opening statement to all my classes was " I expect to be the best teacher you have ever had and I expect you will be the best students I've ever had.".

This statement wasn't presented until I had taught about seven years. By this time my reputation was known and the students knew I meant every word.

When I was the rookie, I copied the control of that period "the paddle". One of my young charges thought he would check me out and became a class problem. I took him in the hall and called to another teacher to witness the swing of "the paddle". After the execution, the student turned to me and asked "Is that all the harder you can hit ? You better find another way !".

I had met with the toughest bottom in the district. He was a pro and considered paddle proof. So we had a long talk about why I was there and what I expected of him. He felt I was reasonable and really cared about doing a good job. The result was unbelievable and we had three very good years together. However, I had to close my door and smile whenever the math teacher down the hall was getting to him with "the paddle".

I had found that when you are honest, treat the student as a young person, show them there is no war and no one is trying to prove anything, then they understand you are the teacher, you make the rules within the

23

classroom and teamwork begins.

The fear in discipline becomes a reflex, instead of the need for discipline to become a tool for learning and self control. If you can have the discipline come from the student instead of your hand, it is less stressful for all concerned. Many times a stern look is enough to convey a message of disappointment or disfavor.

The referral to the office should be used with the student that is a continual problem and is taking up class time.

There are some students that will never care about school or understand what is going on. Let the professionals take over when you have done all you can and work with those who want to learn. We can try, but sometimes we can't see the real problem that those trained to see can.

Party Time: Parties, Rewards and Films

My classes usually understood that I was from the old school and they knew what to expect. Student motivation was in the one to one comment or phrase... "Okay!", " That's it !", "Are you really sure?", or "Look again!". To do well or seek understanding was reward in itself. Every student wants to succeed and his teacher's praise or guidance can only feed his need for more.

Pizza parties for achievement or any other type of party reward is soon forgotten, because it is not a personal goal of learning. I hope we have moved the level of learning beyond that of the dog trainer and the Shamu showman. If not, we can just toss them a treat for doing a trick.. And in reality, parties end up as a day out of class work. I find that flag pole sitting, throwing mud at the Principal, or other forms of demeaning the authority has the same result as parties. Why can't we make school fun without throwing away the reason for being there in the first place.

Showing of movies is more free time, unless you have some way of showing that learning skills are enforced and you can justify a grade. I have known teachers that showed films so the class would be amused, while they made out grades for the semester report card..

There are several good films that can be used to enrich any subject area. They are able to dramatize or show special effects unequaled to anything done in the classroom. There are worksheets, preview materials and further subject references on the web and other films.

Sometimes there are academic rewards or gifts given

by administrators. These are usually in the form of a passing grade or a placement to another grade level or assignment. The reason for or the allowance to is usually a mystery. It is not our place to question, since it is *not* done under our signature. The same follows suit for any dismissal of a student from the school.

Whatever you do for class or individual motivation as an incentive needs to be consistent. It is your class and you are in charge. So keep it uncomplicated and enjoy the class.

As a new and experienced teacher, you will learn lessons daily. Most of the time you will find out how young students think. Usually how inventive they can be. Your job is to listen and see what they are up to.

Jack, for the sake of a name, was a member of my middle school Science Class. He shot off rockets, built planes and flew kites(box type). He liked math and any kind of demonstration I would cook up in lab. He was a real pleasure to have around. He and his buddies cooked up an experiment of their own and kept it a secret.

Jack had made a device that would shut off his air till he passed out. Then when he relaxed the airway opened. Only one time it didn't and Jack was gone.

We did Earth Science demos and nothing that would have given him any idea for his device. But I often thought of Jack and avoided putting any seeds in young minds that could ever be turned into something to regret.

The Coach- Why you are there.

Fear, intimidation, and lack of self confidence are the major problems in student learning. The teacher represents knowledge and enforcement to most students. Many students seem to handle the situation and move in the direction of least resistance—cooperation. However, there are many who have been poorly handled in past learning environments and have shut down to protect their comfort zones, thus developing conflicts and apparent lack of interest in what is going on.

This is where you come in. There must be open lines of communication between you and the student. Ideally this is done on a "one on one basis", but that is a dream in today's classroom. With a full class you have yourself split in your attention. You are thinking of what you're going to say, listening to yourself say it, and watching every face to see if there is recognition of what you just said.

Surprise!, you find blank looks. Then you regroup and start from square one again. By now you realize that you did a good job on your part and it has to be **all** of them. This is the origin of the lounge phrase "The whole class is stupid!". They are afraid to react. They don't want to be wrong in the eyes of their peers or in the mind of the teacher. They want to please.

If you have found a communication block with your students, you may have an intimidating nature that will prevent reaching them. Your next move is to let them know who you really are.

Begin to relax your body language. Don't become

too sloppy, but move about and lean on something to give your stature a less rigid or comfortable line. Laugh at your own mistakes and make little of theirs. Give more common up to date examples to illustrate what you're trying to get across. Use more of the students' terms in your examples.

Save being stern for when the time calls for it. Remain positive in most all interactions till you feel you must assert your authority to maintain order. Always do what you say you will do. They have heard meaningless threats from others before.

I have used some phrases to help make a point for myself or give students some idea of what I expect of my classes.

You may want to use them:

"The word dumb means unable to speak. Therefore a dumb question is never spoken. An honest question deserves an answer."

"If you never try you will never make a mistake. If you make a mistake learn by it ....not make it a habit."

"The teacher is a mirror and can only reflect your attitude and interest. The view is lost if you turn away and so is learning."

"You can do nothing more than your best and only you can make it better."

"If someone is failing don't give them a grade they can't climb out of to pass."

"You must take students as they are, not where you want them to be. Then help them reach the goal you see for them."

It must go two ways... you want them to understand what you expect and your personality...you in turn must be able to reach out and understand their needs and motivation.

One of the best ways is to become part of their extracurricular activities. Talk with them in the lunch room or between classes and see what their interests are and what they enjoy doing. This can be done at any grade level.

I don't expect you to become a buddy and lose the line that is expected to separate the adults from the students. Remember the students expect you to stay on your side also. They want their space. Many times just being there when they are doing something they are happy with and sharing their excitement is all that is needed. Become a good audience so they can show off.
From then on let it be a casual comment in your greeting or informal times.

Coaching sports or helping with school plays and other special activities is always an option. But keep it separate from the classroom. I had a typing teacher who loved sports and would talk for hours with the athletes in his classes. I was a swimmer at the National level and he would daily seek me out during class. I always got an "A" in the class and to this day I type very well.... with two fingers and a thumb.

Be open for any opportunity to be human with your classes. Share with respect both ways by helping them work with adults and still be happy students ready to learn.

While working with a high school swim team, an eleventh grader approached me with a problem. He wanted to be a diver for the school. He had been living in the shadow of his big brother, who had won the city title in High School diving a few years earlier.

He showed me some of the dives he could do. He was working on high point difficult dives and crashing into the water.

"If you can help me with these dives I think I would have a chance for a medal," he said. From what I saw, I could only visualize a potential series of 10 dives with very low scores.

A plan came to mind that would need 10 low point dives that would receive high grades. The grade is the product of the score(1 to 8) times point difficulty (2.0 to 3.0). For the next six weeks Johnny worked on the basic front and back dives that included very few twists and somersaults.

His desire led him to win the City, District and State Championships. The key is to do what you can.... the best you can. There is nothing else you can do. Johnny was pleased and I shared in learning his lesson. Payday!!

R and R: Lounge and Lunchroom

The Teacher's Lounge is an experience all by itself. First remember it is a time and place where a teacher unwinds. Do not take anything said there as being gospel. All the things that a teacher wishes he or she could have said to the class will come out there. It is a good time to get to know the staff and hear some of the gossip.

Usually the lounge has some comfortable furniture, chairs and kitchen table, refrigerator, microwave, telephone, copy machine, and bulletin board. There may be more or less depending upon the school administration. You can depend upon a Sunshine Fund donation annually or semi-annually for whatever comes up that needs cards or flowers. If you bag your lunch, be sure your name is on it. Many times someone will bring in goodies to leave in the middle of the table for all to clean up. Don't be shy, but don't take the last one. One of the pros may have an eye on it.

Watch the time. Try to be one of the first few to class. That way you know you will be back to your room on time. You will always have a few teachers that will drag back to class. They may know something that you don't and you don't want to find out. Every year you will see some new faces and miss some that are not there.

While I was in the Navy, I met many different people with different values. Through time I found that I was attracted to many that shared the same views that I did. Later, I found that I talked and stayed with a few I could trust. You may find the same experience will keep you from making some bad decisions and let you develop into one of the pros that helped you make the decisions to become a teacher. Enjoy your peers, but *be* yourself.

Lunchrooms can come in any form or description. You may have an assignment the first term. Lay back till you know what to expect of the situation and what is really expected of you. You should be put with an experienced teacher.

This is the same as working with special classes. The lunchroom assignments are seldom grouped and your students can be mixed classes, which opens the door for problems you may not be aware could happen.

After the first week, there will be a settling within the group. By this time they are busy with school problems and not spending time looking for conflict. It can turn out to be another opportunity for you to know the students. Stay positive !

Pinch Hitter: The Substitute

It is commonly understood that subs are put into all types of classrooms and they are at the mercy of the teacher of that classroom. If the class feeling is that the teacher is giving students a day off, then you can expect anything to happen with your classroom and any materials therein. However, a good substitute is first of all a teacher. They do not teach content or evaluate students, but work to help students understand the concepts of the class...your class. Therefore, give the sub a plan that will help the sub understand what is happening.

This is a check list that should be followed for a sub:

a) An up-to-date seating chart with marks on the chart and a
   key on the side indicating:
   who will help explain what the class is doing
   who has medical problems(mark as confidential)
   who should not leave the classroom
   who should stay in his/her seat
b) A list of general classroom rules expected of the class.
c) A "NO" list of *never do* rules.(*)
d) The emergency plans for fire etc.
e) How to contact the office or a teacher nearby.(*)(* Hope
   these are never needed)

There are teachers that run a very open and familiar classroom, and there are subs that will never cover such classes again. Meet some of the subs that come to your school and talk with them about what they expect when they cover for you. This way you have some idea which sub you would prefer in your classroom. Talk with the staff person who requests the subs.

Some teachers need a sub only once a year, others need them more frequently. Don't think you are bulletproof, indispensable and will not need a sub. It takes the five years of a new teaching experience to reach that level. Every sort of disease from every home and restroom walks into your class room in one day's time.

If you are a survivor and have been known to dive from a steam bath into a Norway Fiord, you may have a strong immune system(the others died). Normally, an immune system will last for a while, and when it doesn't, stay out till you are all better. If you come back too soon, your second bout will be a longer and a chronic one.

Substitutes know they are good targets for the trouble making student. They don't know the students. They are not sure of the rules or how the teacher runs the class. They may not be back again. The teacher will never know what really happened...so the subs need your support with plans and information. Don't let them down. In return, if you are disappointed in the person who subbed for you don't call them back and tell the administration why. If you let it go by, you're at fault.

The most important tool for everyone is the lesson plan. The length of the plan must always be figured to be longer than the class time. For many very good reasons; something may not be possible to do for various reasons. The books may be misplaced, the room locked, lights are out, your projector is not working and the sub has to improvise to keep the class working. There is something to choose from to alter the plans. If the plans have misjudged the time needed and everyone finished sooner than expected, the sub has something to continue during the class time.

Keep the plans simple. Be sure to give reference titles, page numbers, and items to be covered. You may have someone for a sub that has had little or no training in the area you are working. The sub would just do what is planned and help where it is possible. Professionally, the sub can do the job the best way possible and not lose the day.

Be sure to relate your method of assigning and collecting all work, assume nothing.

The sub is not to evaluate students work, unless you feel the sub is qualified. I wouldn't recommend it at any time. You are the one responsible for giving grades to your student. By law you are the only one accountable.

Have some way that the sub can relate the positive and negative activities of your classes and what was done in each case. Your teaching methods are evaluated by the school's administrators and should not be included in the sub report. Do not be concerned until your administrator says you're in trouble.

The sub should only report class activities and all interactions. You will be responsible to honor the report from the sub and react to the class at your next meeting. If this is done the class will realize it wasn't fun and games, but has value on their grade. You expect to hear good things, and when you don't you are disappointed in their lack of maturity. Praise their efforts whenever you can and call aside the problem students. Talk with them outside the classroom. NEVER punish the whole class by blasting the few during class time.

If the sub has let you down or appeared to dislike working with students, look for someone who enjoys being there and who will motivate the students to work.

I missed a few days of class and heard all sorts of reports from the class about the sub that covered for me. She was unfair, she yelled at the class, she didn't know how to help the class understand what the they were supposed to do. The three days were shot as far as learning was concerned. From what was heard, the sub was the problem.

I checked through the materials from my box in the office and found the complete set of instructions I had left for the sub. Did she ignore my plans and try to wing it on her own? I thought I should give her the benefit of the doubt and called her. She came out to the school that afternoon. Then came the dawn! She didn't understand that she was allowed in my box and didn't receive the plans. She apologized for not asking questions and tried to handle it herself.

From that day on, I had a friend to call on to sub and felt comfortable that the class was in good hands. She in turn knew that detailed plans would be waiting for her when she checked in.

The Play is the Thing: Thinking process.

The one word that begins most any educational process is "Why?". The *Socratic* type teacher's reply is usually another question, "So what do you think?", or something similar that will induce thinking from predetermined information of the questioner.

"Why?" should be answered at the understanding level of the one asking the question. If one of my sons at the third grade in school would have asked me why the light turned off when the bulb burned out.

I *could have* answered by saying that the filament had reached a point where the total resistance overheated the tungsten filament or perhaps the seal at the base of the bulb had allowed the concentration of oxygen to increase in the argon within the bulb and the wire rapidly oxidized. Can you imagine the number of questions that would follow that explanation? (I hope my son would be able to understand my answer now). At the time, I could have answered that the bulb was worn out, like your shoes were last week, and we have to get a new one.

Answers are to be given that allow past learned information to develop an answer that needs one or two new bits of information. You must have an understanding of where the person is now, not where you want him/her to be.

If you are *uncomfortable* with this method of answering, then work out a *progressive* answer. This will give you a chance to direct your strategy toward the best level of understanding. You begin by asking a very broad question on the subject.

If the answer indicates that the subject is familiar, then ask another that will narrow the topic toward the main question. Continue on and add the necessary information as you go. Remember in any case that the process is to help the individual reason inductively or deductively toward the correct answer on his/her own with your assistance. You end up with someone who can work with new understanding, not just a dead bulb.

"I don't know!" is a good answer, when you don't have a clue. You lose all credibility when you try to bluff your way out. Now you have the pleasure of working with someone to find the answer. This is an excellent learning situation. It gives everyone a chance to solve a problem using various research skills from the word Go! You will find that the questioner is supportive to the quest and not ready to point to your ignorance.

Every question should be considered an *honest* question and treated as one, otherwise you will lose the timid individuals.

I am sure that most everyone at sometime has asked a question and may have been intimidated by rejection of some sort, causing interest and inclusiveness to halt.

Your vocabulary is most important in giving an answer. Many sophisticated answers will turn off the average person. The first few words out of your mouth will determine how you will be received by a listener. I usually watch eye contact and other physical body expressions to know if the line of communication is still open. Several years ago, I met with a parent after report card grades were sent home. She couldn't understand why her son had a failing grade for the second grading period.

"You told me that my son was *passing* and now I find he is in trouble," were the first words out of her mouth. I brought out my copies of notes and messages to parents (a good idea to keep records of everything) and relayed back that I said her son was *passive* in my class.

I apologized for not being clear... then gave her some suggestions on how her son could improve.

There are fun ways to begin a class that will instill thought right from the start:

"Did you know that your pencil is evaporating and in a zillion years all that will be left is the lead and the eraser holder?".. "Smell it, your nose can smell the atoms leaving".

"Turn on the dark, It's always here".

"You don't really see me, you just think you do".

"After the Sun goes out, there are 8 minutes of light heading for Earth".

"What verb can you do best?".

"Why is the number line called infinite ?"

There must be some part of the subject you are teaching that would be fun just to toss about and let their minds have fun thinking about it.

I was looking out the classroom window at the clouds rolling by, announcing another day of Ohio snow.

I saw a streak on the pane and it turned out to be a crack. A student with the right swipe on the glass could cut a finger (don't think they wouldn't try).

The custodian said, "We don't fix cracked windows only broken ones."

Later that day I contacted the custodian to tell him that the snow was coming in my broken window.

I had found a gneiss rock to help solve the problem.

Game Plan: Curriculum

The course curriculum is a tentative outline of how the main parts of the program may be implemented. Again, you are the control of the classroom and what is going to be accomplished with your students.

You must have a chance to read and plan the curriculum for your course of study. If no one has a copy of the course of study, you plan as well as you can. Don't jump in and try to plan the first six weeks all at once. Your daily lesson plan book should be setup as far as necessary and you decide what is necessary. There are so many things that can spring up causing you to change plans. I usually planned thoroughly for a week and a half. I made the changes as I went along and tried to keep a comfortable pace. It is also a good idea to keep a log of references along the side of the pages of the plan book.

Some administrators will periodically check your grade and lesson plan books. Speak with your administrator and ask if you can roughly outline future plans and fill in as you change or add to your course. Part of your yearly evaluation will come from their seeing how well you are organized. So communicate as often as you need to and keep those who evaluate you aware of your presence and what is happening. Don't do this during their lunch or without some sort of appointment via the Principal's Secretary.

As I implied before, the curriculum is a tentative outline. When you know your students and have a good hold on the goals of the program, make some changes *that work* and continually help the students understand what is expected of them.

You may find some "arm chairing" as part of the curriculum. This refers to ideas that are dreamt up by the writer that *should* work and generally don't because of an oversight in preparation. So try everything that is questionable before you do it with the class.

Don't become timid, if you are asked to be a member of a writing team. Give it a good try. If you don't do well, they won't ask again. This is a time for you to grow as a teacher and presenter of studies.

It's a great experience, as long as they will use what has been done and not put it on the dusty shelves with other efforts done by your peers. When I have been one of the writers, I have felt that I've contributed to the education of our youth.

One of my science students brought in a Boa Constrictor for the class to see. Not wanting to stifle the interests of science, I said I would be responsible for it for one day only and he had to take it home after school. I was in my fourth year teaching and very much afraid of snakes.

Each period I would bring out the snake and hold him and talk about his structure and let students touch him. I was doing very well with the challenge, until the last period. When I tried to let the snake down, I found that my hand was numb and the snake had my whole arm in a winding grip. Several of the bigger boys came to my rescue. This rookie had learned a lesson never to be forgotten.

Batting Practice: Homework

The more you keep homework a positive feature of your class, the more it will motivate the student to do it well. I know of teachers who have assigned extra work as a punishment for class behavior. No one likes to be punished. Also the same teacher who makes the same individual write a sentence over and over will produce a student who will write very poorly and very little on a homework assignment.

You will spot some of these depressed students as you see the work come in. Give these students special attention and encourage them to loosen up and communicate. In a full class you may have very few contacts with each member and this is a signal for help. All work moving back and forth is like a conversation and many feelings travel with the words from you as well from the student.

You should only make homework assignments when they are necessary. If you are looking for busy work, collect their daily doodling, but if you want progress and learning make all work meaningful and of gradable value.

Hint: Many **copied papers** can be detected by the same misspellings or identical poor phrasing.

As in baseball, you make the calls. It is your judgement that decides the grade and it will not change. Hint #2: Don't set the scale so high or low that you put the student in a no-win position. If they don't see how they can get out of the hole, they will find a way of putting you in a no-win position and you have lost a student who possibly could have learned and made you proud of him.

It's a two way street, Rookie. Grade and return all

papers within a reasonable time. Be sure there is enough time for you to help some of the class understand why they got the grade they did. Don't make an assignment that will make a time problem for you

In the beginning of the year, I made preparing homework a class lesson and went through some possible errors(no names) and how to improve on them. I put complete sentence comments on the sides of homework turned in, especially if I see that they are making an effort.

All of this is slow and frustrating for everyone, but this evaporates as you and the students bond in your efforts to communicate and learn the lessons of the day. You won't change something that has taken years to instill in a student's character, but you sure can chip at it.

A student in my Sociology class received a low grade on his midterm test because his writing was so poor. He turned in his final test at the end of the term with great flourish and gesture. "I typed it this time", says he with a great grin. "That's fine with me", said the professor, "It was quit a feat. Seeing that you typed a 'Blue Book' written test in this room in two hours without using a typewriter. Your answers copied from the 'Frat' files earned you an F ". We didn't really need him on the football team anyhow.

If the plural of goose
  is geese.
Then the plural of moose
  Is meese.
Likewise the plural of mouse
  being mice,
Would certainly call two homes
  a set of hice.

One of the students in my home room went into the gym locker of another student and took his gym shoes.
He proudly wore them to school the next day and was seen by the boy who had the shoes originally. I was called into the office with both students. I asked the boy why he took the shoes. He said ,
"My parents can't afford to get shoes for me, but his parents can get him another pair."
It was an answer I never expected.
The school bought him his own pair and he gave the others back to the student that owned them. With a warning about taking things that belong to others. It is a good idea to have some source of help to prevent this sort of thing from happening again.

In my second year of teaching, I taught 12th grade Science in a suburb of Cleveland. It was a very smart class and all were A and B students. One day I was collecting homework and one of the girls hadn't done it. I gave my usual pitch about homework being a second chance to learn the lesson of the day. I turned and she was in tears. I couldn't understand what I had done to cause her reaction. Her best friend motioned me to one side and informed that she had a crush on me.

After that lesson I had a bigger one at the end of the semester. The class decided that they had enough points to pass my course with D's and C's and were not going to do any more work. From then on we held study hall and I put the daily Science assignments on the board, which they ignored for the rest of the year.

When report cards came out, there were 22 seniors not graduating because they had gotten an incomplete for a Science grade. The principal held class during the Summer and used my lesson plans to give late credit and finally their diplomas.

Fellow rookies, I made sure I was traded for the next year to another school system.

At Bat: Testing

There are several ways of testing a student to see if they understand the material covered in your class. There must be care taken in the type of student you are testing. Circumstances may make your test invalid. Here are some things to be considered:

a) The reading level of the student. Guidance may have overlooked something in placing someone in your class who may be over achieving and could reach their potential short of your testing. A new teacher will usually find this out over the first three or four tests given. The usual reaction from the teacher is, "The whole class is stupid !". Many students will do well as long as the material is spoken, but the test is based on reading skill not listening and they lose it.

b) Your vocabulary. You, as the teacher, must be careful not to use some of your own past learning in test preparation and hit them with terms that are not used in the information they have received. In fact you may want to use some of their terms in preparing the question. They will be impressed with your versatility.

c) Use the test form that will allow the most feedback:

1. Matching is excellent for recalled recognition. This is done with two vertical columns of terms. The first column of terms is numbered, each preceded with a space for a letter answer. The second column is lettered from A to ? and each contains a matching short definition. The object is to match the term with the best definition. DO NOT have the same number of definitions as terms, use a

couple more. This way they will never be sure if they are just putting down answers. (I like them to guess and truly think through a possibility if they are not sure. A blank answer is a wrong one in any case.)

2. Multiple Choice is another mental exercise in making good decisions. There should be four choices. One is the correct answer, the second is called the "foil". It could be right if something were different. The third is wrong for a good reason, and the last has no relation to the question in any way.
(Avoid using " none of these" or "all of these" as the fourth choice. Unless the answer is obvious and you want to give a couple of helping points).

3. True and False will give a fifty - fifty chance to be wrong. Be careful of the wording when making the questions. "All or Never" are usually false indicators and many things can be read into the rest of the questions and phrases. These are the hardest questions to write, so be sure of your words and meanings.

4. Completion questions are for the students who have memorized the material and will give an answer close to what you want or have read the phrase another way and still could be counted right. Don't try to be clever with this type of question. Call it as it is and double check your phrasing. When you grade these read the answer carefully... they may not see it as you wanted it to be.

5. Essay questions can lead to an understanding of the ability of the student to communicate by written word. You will see how they express themselves in relating to your subject. Keep your questions short and simple.

The important thing is whether they are afraid of making a mistake and say very little or open up with trust and spill all and hope you understand them. If they trust that you will not put them down for being stupid, they will try their best. Otherwise you will never know what they have gleaned from being in your classroom.(This is where I learned the most about my ability as a teacher).

6. Charts, Maps and Graphs–Oh, My! These are to be done in the clearest fashion possible. Check to see if they have been duplicated correctly and clearly. I can not emphasize this enough. Always be professional and your students will reflect your professionalism in their efforts in return. Make the questions short and all responses in letter or number form.

You are the evaluator of your students. You decide what their grade value is in testing. This is really a small part of evaluating the whole student. If you find that this is the only data in your evaluation, I feel you are short as a "Complete Teacher". Go after a thorough evaluation.

There are so many ways to cheat on a test that it would take many more pages to cover the methods. I dislike the newspapers when they give the M.O. of a crime or how to make an explosive and I don't want to pass any ideas on to the ignorant. So my approach will be how to prevent it.

I.   Rearrange the order of the pages
II. Don't use answer sheets.

III. Don't use old tests.
IV. Assign seats in a staggered pattern.
V. Only what is needed is allowed in reach.
   (Store books etc. in back of room).
VI. Purses and loose valuables in the front of the room.
VII Nothing carried in or out during breaks.

Dead give-aways:
   Shading their eyes while propping head.
   Dropping something on the floor.
   Keeping scrap paper after test.

It is especially nice when you know your class and can trust them. This is the best way. You become paranoid if you watch for cheating.

Designated hitter: Special Classes

There are some special classes you may be asked to teach. These classes are grouped by student readiness, advanced or basic programs, or being physically or mentally challenged. In any case, your class will have students to be taught subject material differently than the "regular class".

There are teachers who are trained to work with students placed in these special classes. Sometimes these specially trained people are not available and you are asked to step in. You will be given the necessary materials to work on with the class and directions concerning how they expect you to teach.

If you're still at the rookie stage and very unsure of what is expected of you, don't try to work it out for yourself. Yell and kick till you get someone's attention. Everyone in the school is doing their own thing and will feel everything is going well with you, if they don't hear anything. Communication is the key word for all rookies. Help is usually close at hand and ready.
A good administrator is looking ahead and should have a good idea of how to help you.

Never become frustrated and take it out on the students. By now they know whether you're on task or not and they will do their best to help you make the adjustment. They were always there for me. In reality, you will work things out together in *your own way*. A course of study is not set in stone. If you make a mistake, fix it and move on. You and your class can form a bond that will follow you the rest of your teaching days. So make it a pleasant time for everyone.

I taught chemistry and physics. One year I was asked to teach a basic math course to a group that the teachers' lounge called "Indians". They were! However, after a few days of survival, I realized these students had been put together as a group because of general ability for years, and success was not a word related to math.

I introduced an unfamiliar game to them and challenged them to figure it out.
I used the term "War of the Kings" and set up a chess board. I explained the pieces and what they were able to do to capture the king without being taken by the enemy first. With the help of several other chess sets, we played for a week. Then I dropped the other shoe.

" Hey guys !" says I, "Hold up on the wars !". By this time they realized they were playing one of those smart games and were enjoying the success. From then on they were allowed to play every Friday, IF they had finished their work for the week and were passing. They did! For many years after the class, some of the students from that class would yell "check" as we would pass in the hall. My payday was when the graduating members from that class of "Indians" stood at the close of the ceremonies and yelled "Check !".

The Majors:The Complete Teacher

The term "Complete", meaning all inclusive, is a bit hard to pin on a person. To attain it is a matter of personal evaluation. You can not design yourself to be a complete teacher... it comes with "being there". I believe many of us can look back and pick out one or more teachers who have been special in our lives. They have been there when you needed encouragement. They were there at special times in your life like graduation or marriage, or they were there when your life was falling apart and you didn't think you were going to make the grade or reach some of your goals. Then time passed. If you met them on the street or talked with a friend and the name came up, you had the feeling that person was "my teacher". (pay day !)

Being a teacher is a special charge. You find yourself given more and more responsibility as a person to a person. It happens in the classroom or passing in the hallway. You will find that just being there with a smile and ready to go to work is enough.
Sometimes you will say things kind of off the top of your head and go on with the lesson.

You represent what the young people can expect of the their future. So many are insecure of what life will bring to them and here is someone talking about things to prepare them for their future... someone who really wants them to have a good life. They see the future through your eyes and understand that you have done well. They feel confident that your information will help them .

A teacher is not a doctor or psychologist. You can not solve problems that need the professional's help. Keep the invisible wall foremost when working with young people. Use good sense in talking with them. Never talk with any student without an adult witness. Stand in the doorway during class passing. Meet no students after hours unless supervised. Never meet with a parent about a student unless you are in an administrator's office with the administrator present.

Protect yourself every minute. There have been teachers accused of many things that may not have happened. Even those cleared have been marked by the incident. Don't trust anyone! However, if your chances of being there for your students were successful, you evaluated each student on what they did to their ability. You did your job to the best of your ability as you learned more of what you could do. You remained honest to your students in your efforts to help them understand that they control what they will be. You can thank the Lord and put your head down to sleep at night and understand what it has taken for you to be complete.

My note: Students from the past have come back to my classroom or met me in a store or someplace and have related that I had said something that meant a great deal to their life. Even after they told me what it was, I don't remember ever saying it. But was pleased that I had.

Keeping in Shape- and the job.

One of the common problems in the teaching field is keeping up with teacher expectations. You are expected to be current in your skills as a teacher.

Much of your time has been spent on the instructor's side of the desk. Now you need time on the learner's side. Your school system will inform you of the requirements to renew your state teaching certificate or local credits. Usually you have a period of so many years to complete the requirements. Don't wait!

You presently have a certain level of subject or grade level certification that you may want to change or take courses for a higher degree. Some teachers may have been hired to teach a subject out of their field and have a very short time to get the necessary credits to keep their job. This will take a lot of thought and advice from your school system along with time and money.

Many teachers will have a second job or decide to coach a sport or activity for needed funds.

Coaching will pay according to the sport. Football and Basketball are the better paying because they have admission charged for their games to supplement their budget. The minor sports like Swimming, Track, and Cross Country depend on the school budget to survive.

Your school system will offer workshops and other in-house type of enrichment to help build up credits needed throughout the year, however, these workshops and other credits are to be collected outside of the school day.

The NEA and other such teaching organizations will give opportunities for extended education during the Summer months. You may even find some colleges that will give Summer programs for credit also. Check these out and you might find help with the cost for teachers.

After so many years of experience, some systems will allow a sabbatical leave for educational purposes. I received one when the National Science Foundation granted me a scholarship to get my Master's Degree.

There are ways of maintaining your professional status, but no one is to going to seek you out. You have to let your needs be known... good and loud. Work with your professional organizations, that's why they are there. Higher education instructors are faced with a "publish or parish" syndrome. They will be out of work if they don't keep themselves in professional shape

Runs, Hits, and Errors: Notes

Principal _____

School _____

School Telephone _____

School Secretary _____

Nurse _____

Absent or Late Call-in Number _____

Schedule:

_____   _____

_____   _____

_____   _____

_____   _____

_____   _____

_____   _____

_____   _____

<u>Notes</u>

Runs, Hits, and Errors: Notes

Counselor _____

Custodian _____

Teacher Aide(s) _____

_____

Future Substitute(s) _____

_____

Other Important People:

_____ _____

_____ _____

_____ _____

_____ _____

Notes

<u>Runs, Hits, and Errors: Notes</u>

First Day of School _____

Thanksgiving Break _____
Return _____

Christmas Break _____
Return _____

Easter Break _____
Return _____

Last Day With Students _____

<u>Other important dates</u>

_____ _____
_____ _____
_____ _____
_____ _____
_____ _____
_____ _____
_____ _____
_____ _____
_____ _____
_____ _____
_____ _____
_____ _____
_____ _____
_____ _____

61

Notes

<u>Runs, Hits, and Errors: Notes</u>

Be sure you have signed all insurance papers.

Know where all sign- in sheets are posted.

Locate the teachers bulletin board and be familiar with the location and the monthly contents of all Departmental and/or Superintendent's Bulletins.

Locate the teachers' and administrators' message boxes.

Talk with other teachers and representatives of Local and State Teacher Associations. Read and understand <u>everything</u> before you sign.

Best of Luck, Rookie !

Order Form

Number of Copies _____
of Classroom Rookie

Price per copy: $8.50
    Florida Residents include Florida Sales Tax
    or Tax Exempt Certificate Copy

    Book Cost Total   _____

Postage and Handling _____(will adjust for larger orders)
    1-4 Books-$2.00, add $.50 for each additional.

      Total Amount Due $_____

Name _____

Address _____

City, State, Zip _____

Mail to: Bread and Butter Press
           1107 Dorothy Street
           Lakeland, Florida
           33815-4418
or Call: 1-800-354-2757 or (863) 683-1775
          Fax: (863) 802 3725